THE LIFE COACH'S
TOOLBOX

How to help you help others TODAY

BY ERIC GILSTON

ISBN: 978-1-9996797-0-5

First published 2018

Copyright © 2018 Eric Gilston.

All rights reserved. Apart from any permitted use under UK copyright law, no part of this publication may be reproduced or transmitted in any form or by any means, electronic or mechanical, including photocopying, recording, or any information, storage or retrieval system, without permission in writing from the publisher or under licence from the Copyright Licensing Agency Limited. Further details of such licenses (for reprographic reproduction) may be obtained from the Copyright Licensing Agency Ltd, Saffron House, 6-10 Kirby Street, London EC1N 8TS.

To Whom it May Concern

Ref: Mrs Suzanne F Gortler – Godalming Town Council

I have worked for Godalming Town Council for 8 years and had reached the point at where I needed to have some serious coaching about how to move myself forward. My line manager and the Councillors agreed that I could undertake training with Eric on a 1-1 basis. From the moment I sat with Eric, he understood my stumbling blocks, he listened and was able to provide practical and real-time strategies that have helped me enormously in the last (nearly a year) since I undertook my coaching with him. His coaching session and subsequent catch up discussions since the initial coaching have been invaluable to me. What I have learned from Eric has improved my professional outlook to such a degree that I have just been offered and accepted a large promotion within my organisation.

I feel that this might not have readily been offered if I had continued without Eric's Coaching.

I am grateful to Eric and hope that everyone might have the benefit of his coaching as it really has made a difference.

Thank you Eric.

Suzie Gortler
(Was Projects Coordinator for Godalming Town Council, will be undertaking the Communications Officer and Community Services Officer Role in two months)

CONTENT

Foreword .... 7 - 12

CHAPTER 1. Introduction .... 13 - 16

CHAPTER 2. What about me? .... 17 - 19

CHAPTER 3. Early days of coaching .... 21 - 24

CHAPTER 4. What is Life Coaching? .... 25 - 27

CHAPTER 5. Who needs coaching? 29

5.1. What about a Business Person? .... 30 - 31

5.2. What about Managing Directors & CEOs? 31

5.3. What about Parents? .... 32 - 33

5.4. What about Sports People? .... 33 - 36

5.5 What about a Teacher? .... 37 - 38

CHAPTER 6. Leading up to the Toolbox .... 39 - 41

CHAPTER 7. Eric's Coaching Style – **THE TOOLBOX** 43

7.1. The 'Want' Tool .... 44 - 45

7.2. The 'Probing' Tool .... 45 - 48

7.3. The 'Marks Out Of Ten' Tool .... 48 - 51

7.4. The 'Timing' Tool .... 51 - 54

7.5. Summary at this stage .... 54 - 55

7.6. The 'Negative Issues' Tool .... 55 - 58

7.7. The 'Ranking' Tool .... 59 - 61

7.8. The 'One Liner' Tool.. 61 - 62

7.9. The 'My Experience' Tool.. 62 - 63

7.10. The 'Anchor' Tool .... 64 - 65

7.11. The 'Mindset' Tool.. 66 - 68

7.12. The 'Benefits' Tool .... 69 - 71

7.13. The 'Mentoring while Coaching' Tool .... 71 - 73

7.14. The 'Affirmations' Tool .... 73 - 75

7.15. The 'Empathy' Tool .... 75 - 77

CHAPTER 8. A Full Coaching Session .... 79 - 82

CHAPTER 9. Future Opportunities 83

9.1. Sport...84

9.2. Schools 85

CHAPTER 10. Testimonials .... 87 - 92

CHAPTER 11. Eric's One-Liners... 93 - 97

CHAPTER 12. In Conclusion .... 99 - 104

FOREWORD

When Eric asked me if I would be prepared to write a Foreword for his book I was delighted. I have known Eric for 17 years and his passion for coaching and devotion to helping others develop and grow is incredible. He himself has been on a remarkable journey, and through his coaching has helped countless other people. So when he decided to write this book and put his thoughts on paper and share his tools, techniques and methods I was extremely pleased. It now means that other people can benefit from Eric's insights and wisdom.

As someone who has been involved in the world of coaching for over 20 years and currently runs coach training schools in 31 countries, I have seen how coaching crosses borders, cultures, languages and beliefs. I have seen the real power of coaching in action. I have experienced first-hand the difference that true coaching brings to lives, organisations and teams; how it changes individuals and turns managers into leaders, how it demonstrates the real beneficial difference between telling and asking. It really is the difference between force versus power. Coaching lives on the side of power and is all about empowering individuals, helping them to take back true control of their lives and their futures.

As coaching is growing exponentially around the world more and more corporations are embracing it, and thousands of people every year are choosing to work as a Coach. There has never been a greater need for coaches to understand more about their industry, their role and how to work effectively with clients. Unfortunately, standards of training can vary drastically and there are many 'Diploma Mills'; unscrupulous schools and organisations that give people as little as two or three days training and tell them that they can now call themselves a professional coach! Therefore a book like this which gives people true guidance and helps to set them down the right road is invaluable.

This Book GIVES.

This book enables a clear understanding of what coaching is, a brief history of where it started, and the sort of people that need it.

So what exactly is coaching? - Here is a good definition.

"Coaching is about performing at your best through the individual and private assistance of someone who will challenge, stimulate and guide you to keep growing."

Essentially it is about helping you to reach self-actualisation - a point at which you not only truly know yourself but within this knowledge possess a feeling of comfort with and understanding of the person you discover.

Your coach engages in a collaborative alliance with you to establish and clarify purpose and goals and to develop a plan of action to achieve those goals. They will establish an understanding of what is really important to you in life and subsequently enable you to take charge of your life; to construct and act upon action plans that will help you to realise these priorities. Put simply, coaching is about helping you to create and work towards the grandest version of the greatest personal vision you have; to achieve success - success being the continuous realisation of a worthy goal or ideal.

You will be guided through a detailed process beginning with the need to re-evaluate your present position, who you really are, where your priorities lie and the need to make a definite and conscious decision about the future you would like to create. With the help of a personal life coach you really can re-shape your life, overcome all the obstacles and live the life that you love.

Coaching is essentially a conversation - that is, a dialogue between you and your coach. Within a productive, results-oriented context, coaching involves coaching you to access what you already know. The reality is that you have the answers to all your questions - asked and unasked. Your coach provides the essential assistance, support and encouragement to seek and find these answers; to guide you towards asking the right questions, and deal with the answers.

Coaching also incorporates learning and yet a coach is not a teacher and will not necessarily know how to do things better than you but this does not matter. Your coach will observe patterns - set the stage for new actions and then work with you to put these new, more successful actions into place. This involves learning through various coaching techniques such as listening, reflecting, asking questions and providing information. Finally, and most importantly, your coach will help you learn how to become self-correcting and self-generating. That is, you will learn how to correct your own behaviour, generate your own questions and find your own answers.

The 3 main Pillars of Coaching are

In what we call 'pure coaching' there are three main fundamentals, or pillars. These are: be Non Judgmental, Non Directional and, most importantly, and most importantly Coaches have No Answers

This book follows these principles and will guide any coach, no matter what their level of expertise, down the road that will allow them to work successfully with their clients.

Simple and effective TOOLS

All coaches need tools and when you first embark on a career as a Coach having a professional set of tools to lean on, just like a crutch, is invaluable.

This book provides just that - a wonderful set of tools, techniques and methods that a Coach can immediately implement with their Coachee and start to see results very quickly.

The world of Coaching needs more people like Eric Gilston.

Gerard O'Donovan

CEO and Founder of Noble Manhattan coaching Ltd

CEO and founder of International Coaching News

CEO and founder of Boardroom Coaching

CEO of the -International Regulator for Coaching and Mentoring

Follow me on Twitter

http://twitter.com/gerardodonovan

Read my Blog at

http://www.gerardodonovan.com/blog

CHAPTER 1

—

INTRODUCTION

It was during a conversation, to someone who wanted to know more about coaching, that the concept of a 'life coach's toolbox' came to mind.

There I was, meeting up with her once a week, and going through various case studies of mine, when she suddenly said, *"Eric, it sounds like you have this toolbox, and depending on what the issue is that someone has, you pull out another tool from your toolbox".* The idea of a book was born at that moment.

Since qualifying as a Life Coach in January 2001 through the then Life Coaching Academy, I have coached many young people, both on a one-to-one basis and in groups. I have also coached many adults, including a Headteacher and teachers.

As a coaching session develops, I have learned over time that **a good coach is one who must have two key qualities,** viz. that of being a good listener, as well as one who can ask good questions.

Based on these two qualities, the coach then needs to know that they have a 'toolbox', from which they can pick out the appropriate 'tool' to help the coachee move forward to a satisfactory solution to their issue. There is no standard solution, as each issue is unique, and will require the coach having a full 'toolbox' from which to select the appropriate 'tool' at each appropriate moment throughout the coaching session.

It is therefore my intention to show, within this book, the various tools that I have used over the past 17 years, and relate them to real situations that have arisen during coaching sessions. In this way, this book will be a great help, not only to life & business coaches, but also to anyone working with someone to resolve issues they are facing, **when a new approach might just be what is needed to change the thinking of the coachee.**

Here are just a few examples of where the toolbox could prove invaluable.

- A parent talking to their child, but not getting their message across and needing to try a different approach.
- What about a teacher talking to one of their students and needing to try something different?
- It could even be the Headteacher wanting to talk to a member of their staff about something personal.
- What about all sports coaches wanting to say the same thing they have been saying for many years, but now having a different way to say it, and maybe getting a different result and/ or a different reaction?
- It will also be invaluable to any business, for anyone needing to coach a member of staff at all levels, but can't afford to pay for a qualified life or business coach.

The value of coaching someone, and the reward, is immeasurable. However, when someone writes a testimonial, you realise just what you have done for them. So, I have included, later on in this book, a selection of testimonials that I have received over the years in order to inspire you to start as quickly as possible, and coach that first lucky person.

You might be thinking "why is Eric writing this book and giving away his knowledge and techniques that he has acquired over the past 17 years?" The answer is simple. I am absolutely passionate, not only about the subject of coaching, but also how it can be used to change people's lives. I therefore want to give as many people as possible the opportunity to use what I have used, and help people who have issues, get them resolved in such a way that their lives will be changed. That's why.

If you are also thinking whether or not you could do coaching, then just start by thinking about whether or not you are the person who helps their friends or relations with solving issues, or are you the person people turn to when they have a problem? If this describes you, then you have the makings of becoming a coach.

Please note that this book is **NOT** about helping you to build a coaching practice. It is also **NOT** filled with the Theory of Coaching, but instead it will provide you with many of my Practical thoughts and actions.

Hopefully, this book will become my legacy for many, many years to come, and I will hear people say that they are using the "Eric Gilston way of coaching".

CHAPTER 2

—

WHAT ABOUT ME?

I am blessed. I have been lucky enough to have found my purpose in life. Have you?

To be able to help people of all ages, especially teenagers, to move forward with their lives, by using the power of coaching, is hard to describe. Suffice to say, it has been the most rewarding time of my life – so far – but there's lots more for me to achieve. See the section later on in this book, titled Future Opportunities.

In fact I am writing this part of the book while on holiday in Carvoeiro, in the Algarve, Portugal, but at the same time **looking forward to the next group of students that I will be coaching** at a school, one-to-one, the day after I return to London. This is why I have a passion for coaching. Is it self-satisfaction? Or, looking at it from the student's point of view, is it a time for them to reflect on how to make positive changes to their lives and move forward on the journey to reach their true potential? For me, it has to be the latter.

Recently I was working with a group of adults, all over 50, and coaching them to get back into paid employment. Imagine my joy when I received a text message, while in Carvoeiro, that read, *"Hi Eric, I tried to call as I wanted to thank you personally for your support over the past few months and for your inspiration."* The text went on to tell me that she had found a job. This is another reason why I love coaching – the reward of hearing good news from people that I have coached.

I suppose that it was inevitable that I would eventually be focusing only on a coaching career. Let me take you back to the 1970's when I qualified as a Football Association Coach & Referee. I then used the coaching qualification to manage a number of teenage football teams as well as a few adult football teams, in my spare time. I can honestly say that all my teams were successful, and in hindsight, I believe that this was due to, not only being tactically aware, but also I was able to talk to my players in such a way that it made them believe in their own abilities, and motivated them to want to be successful, and they were.

I remember being at an award ceremony for young sports people, where my son was one of the nominated candidates for his table tennis prowess, when my wife, my son & I were approached by one of my ex football players, then in his 30s. He turned to my son and said that as a player, he and his team mates didn't appreciate all I had done for them as individuals, and as a team, until I left their club. **What a compliment!** He then went on to say that he was now managing a team of teenagers, and using the techniques that I had used. **My football legacy.**

CHAPTER 3

—

EARLY DAYS OF COACHING

So what got me to think about getting a life coaching qualification? I was with a friend one Saturday morning, and things were not going too well for her at work. As the Managing Director of a company, she was under a lot of pressure and concerned about the possibility of losing her job, and the consequences of the loss of income and the possible change to her lifestyle.

We spoke for quite a while, and without realising it, I was actually coaching her, by asking her some key questions about things that she had not thought about, and also just listening to her talking, that in turn provoked some more questions from me.

Following on from this conversation, or was it my first coaching session, she invited me into her office every Saturday morning to discuss what had happened the previous week and what was going to happen the following week. In actual fact, I was being used as a sounding board for her thoughts, due to the fact that as the Managing Director she did not really have someone within the company to play this role.

It was based on this experience, and the fact that I had loved the interaction so much; I decided that I couldn't do this type of work without a qualification. So, in 2000 I enrolled on a coaching course with the then Life Coaching Academy. During this time, I was exceedingly lucky in being coached by some top coaches including Gerard O'Donovan and Nic Rixon, who were both pivotal in getting me fixed on knowing that this was a great profession to get involved in, and one that I would love dearly, as I would be helping others move forward with their lives.

Soon after I had qualified as a coach in January 2001, I was lucky enough to come across Thomas Leonard, who was the Founder of Coaching. He lived in the USA, and so all of my communications with him were online. Back in 2001 he created a Research Committee that I was fortunate to serve on. Thomas was a creative genius, and each new thought required the input from his Committee members.

This was so inspirational for me, in my first year of coaching, being involved with hearing about brand new coaching thoughts from Thomas Leonard, followed by thoughts from coaches around the world, who were also members of his Research Committee, and then Thomas collating all those thoughts into a new way forward for Coaching.

When Thomas came over to London, I was able to meet with him personally, but unfortunately the world of coaching lost a great man when he sadly passed away in 2003 at the tender age of only 47. His work still lives on, and if you want to learn from the greatest, then check out some of his writings. You will not be disappointed. Rest in peace Thomas.

In fact, I've been checking my files, as I'm a terrible hoarder, and found lots of work from Thomas that would be of immense value to coaches today. Here are some examples:-

- Sometimes the client has the answer; Sometimes the coach.
- How do you coach a friend without messing up the friendship?
- What do you do when you get your first 'real' client?

- How do you coach an entrepreneur with a zillion balls in the air?
- How do you respond to the client who just isn't getting what you're saying?

Pulling all of this together, you can see that I was one very fortunate coach, who had the perfect start to my coaching career by having just over two years of working with the Founder of Coaching, the late great Thomas Leonard. You are sorely missed. What might have been?

CHAPTER 4

—

WHAT IS LIFE COACHING?

A lot of clients I get are referrals from other people that I have coached. However, the majority do not really understand what life coaching is, and require me to explain it to them.

So this is what I say, and it may or may not differ to what other life coaches say. Also, some coaches may agree or disagree with what I say, but then we do not want to produce identical coaches. People deal with people, and need to find the coach that is right for them.

I tell future clients that life is made up of the past, the present and the future, and that I am not going to spend my time discussing their past, but we can learn things from it. However, **my focus throughout our coaching sessions will be on taking them from the present to the future, and where they want to get to.**

A definition of coaching that I like is:- ***Coaching is not a prescription with set answers for every situation. It is about encouraging your client to expand on their thoughts and feelings and, in so doing, they will develop their own strategies for dealing with a given issue. You are there to help in this process and then to help them evolve their own tactics and actions that will bring those strategies into reality. Once evolved, you will keep a supportive pressure on to ensure that the actions are taken.***

Another more simplistic one that I also like is:-***Coaching is the art of facilitating the performance, learning & development of another.*** (Downey 2003)

To date I have coached people both Internationally and in the UK, by phone, Skype & online. However, **my personal preference is face-to-face**, and this tends to take place in the UK. In this instance I give the client the options of the coaching sessions taking place in their home, in my home or at a neutral location.

You might also find another fact very strange. To date I have not made any videos or DVD's, as I want to be able to interact with my clients. **The face to face coaching allows me to look at their eyes when they are talking, to see if the words being emitted from the mouth are in congruence with what their eyes are telling me.**

I remember coaching at one school with a group of 14 year old girls, when I told them that I learn more from someone's eyes than what comes out of their mouth. One young girl immediately said, "Now I know why my mum knows when I'm telling the truth or not". Your eyes are a giveaway.

My priority is always the person being coached. Hence, a teenager might not want to be coached at home, while a business person might prefer somewhere neutral, away from both their home and their office. So, **prior to starting any series of coaching sessions, make sure that you talk to your potential client about all of these options.**

CHAPTER 5

—

WHO NEEDS COACHING?

5.1. What about a BUSINESS PERSON?

In any business, there is a need to improve the performance of all employees, from the lowest paid person right through to the CEO in the company.

There are two ways in which coaching can be applied in any business:-

1. By getting some members of staff to get coached by a qualified Life Coach, and then use their new found knowledge to create a system in the company where those who need coaching can get some.
2. By employing a qualified Life Coach to come into a company and coach employees as and when the need arises as seen by their boss.

There are pros and cons for both options, but in my opinion, every company needs coaching for members of their staff.

There will always be situations where an employee is not meeting the standards required, or not achieving the goals that have been set for them. It is one thing for their boss to talk to them, and make suggestions, but a great coaching session will result in the employee coming up with what could be done to improve their performance. Using this approach will result in the employee feeling empowered to go away and make the necessary changes. This is far stronger than being told what to do, or in the worst case scenario, losing their job.

What about the CEO or Chairman preparing to have a Board Meeting and needing to discuss some very key issues? Who can they bounce their ideas off, and discuss alternative approaches? A non judgemental coach could be the ideal solution.

5.2. What about MANAGING DIRECTORS and CEOs?

What about the CEO and Managing Directors of companies preparing to have a Board Meeting and needing to discuss some very key issues? Who can they bounce their ideas off, and discuss alternative approaches? A non judgemental coach could be the ideal solution.

As I stated in Chapter 3 when talking about what made me think about a career in coaching. It all started when helping a Managing Director review her previous week and plan her following week.

Imagine having someone, independent of the company, who you can use as your sounding board, to bounce all your ideas off, and discuss all the what-ifs, prior to going in to a Board Meeting. Your confidence will be sky high, and you will be ready to answer any questions being fired at you from members of your Board.

Who could you coach, using the tools from this book, to take on this role, who you can trust to keep your discussions confidential and be non-judgemental when meeting with you?

5.3. What about PARENTS?

Over my 17 fabulous years of coaching, I must have coached a few thousand students, both individually, and in classes in schools, from the age of ten through to University age of around 20. I can honestly say that I get immense pleasure from working with these young people, especially when there is a real desire to move forward with their lives.

In all cases, it would have been nice if their parents could have helped them, but I am so grateful that they were not equipped with the right tools to do so, and also, children will listen more to others than they will their own parents. In hindsight, I now know that I was one of those parents.

I therefore hope that, as I will not be able to work with every student throughout the world, then this book will help many parents help their children move forward with issues that they are facing, and for which their children will then be eternally grateful.

It is therefore critical that parents pay particular attention to Chapter 7, and not only start to learn the various tools, but also start to think about some of the issues that their children are currently facing, and which particular tools are most appropriate. They should then try to have a 'mock' coaching session with their child. A couple of key points to note:-

- Don't tell your child that they are going to have a coaching session with you. Just include it in one of your conversations.

- Don't beat yourself up if it doesn't go to plan. Remember that we all had to start somewhere, at some time, and that we learn more from failure than we do success.

5.4. What about SPORTS PEOPLE?

During my 17 years of coaching, I have helped quite a number of sports people progress to achieve bigger goals than they would have done without the coaching.

To date I have coached rugby players, swimmers, rowers and cricketers, all in their teenage years. I would like to add table tennis, as I coached my son when he first took up the sport at the age of 10, but I soon realised that he needed a mentor initially, more than a life coach, to actually teach him the technical and tactical side of the sport.

It was only after I qualified as a life coach, which was seven years after my son started playing, that I realised how badly I had spoken to him both in preparing him mentally for matches, advising him during games, and then having a go at him after matches he lost, and it was most definitely not coaching. How I wished that I had qualified as a coach **BEFORE** he took up table tennis. However, the mentoring that he received was the best, and he became a National Champion at the age of 14.

Back to those sports people that I did coach. In all cases they had issues that needed to be addressed, and required them to determine the solutions that were acceptable, in order for them to move forward. The coaching process that I adopted helped them to do just that, and progress within their chosen sport.

In the case of the rugby players, let me tell you about two of them. I was asked to coach a 16 year old who wanted to get into the USA National Under 17 team, and needed to build his confidence before the trials back in the States, which were only one month away. The approach that I used included using a number of tools that will be described later on in this book. Suffice to say that not only did this 16 year old get chosen for the USA team but I was privileged to go and watch him make his debut against Canada at Millfield School in Somerset. As a coach, the feeling that one has when you see the end result of something that you have worked on is priceless, especially when parents and Grandparents are there from the USA to watch.

The other rugby player received his first coaching session from me when he was only eleven years old, and needed to build his confidence. The tools that were used for this young person were similar to those used for the other rugby player. Roll the clock forward nine years and imagine my delight when on holiday in Carvoeiro, mentioned earlier in this book, I received a text from the mother of this 20 year old to say that he was making his debut that day for the Norwegian National Team playing against Estonia. His dream had come true. (N.B. His mother is Norwegian). A later message informed me that his team had won 43 – 16. Of course you can imagine how I felt. Yet again, the Power of Coaching showed its face. Please note that I am not taking any credit for the tactical and technical coaching that he received over the years or the total dedication that he gave to his sport.

In both of these cases I am not saying that their eventual successes were down solely to coaching, but it most certainly played a part in their eventual key goals being achieved.

In the case of the swimmers, the girls I coached were already competing in National Championships and getting coaching from swimming coaches. However, what I discovered was that the focus of **the coaching that they were receiving was primarily on technique but not on mindset**. From a life coaching perspective this was great, as it opened up lots of additional coaching that I could offer to complement what their sports coach was doing with the girls.

I therefore focused on where coaching could help when they were training, so that what they did then could be replicated when they actually competed in races, and where actions then became habits. This included talking about what they did before they actually reached the pool, e.g. listening to particular music versus just thinking about the race itself, their body language when walking to the pool, e.g. how a confident person walks but not arrogant, etc.

Another interesting point that arose, based on asking some key questions, was where the emphasis was being placed by the swimming coach, in this instance, as regards the importance of winning races. As a life coach I discovered that for the girls that I was coaching, improving their PB (Personal Best) on any occasion resulted in making them feel really great about a performance. Food for thought, for the technical coach – in my opinion. This is not to say that there are not some swimming coaches out there who don't focus on a swimmers PB. Asking a coachee about their feelings at any point of the coaching when they either achieve, or do not achieve something, truly adds to the make up of a great coaching session.

In the case of the rower I coached, he had aspirations for being part of the GB squad, but felt that he was being excluded from being given the chance. As a life coach, this situation opens up a number of options, starting with asking some key questions, and then using some of the tools that you will soon be reading about in this book.

I will go into more detail on Page 73 as to one part of how I helped this particular young man get into the squad.

In the case of a cricketer I coached, she was trialling out for the England Under 19 team. The process in this instance was coaching by email. She would let me know when there was a training session for the squad and we would exchange her goals for that session with an exchange of emails as to all the options that were available to her to achieve her goals. In all instances, I recall her either achieving or exceeding her goals. The actual techniques that were used, from my 'toolbox', will be discussed later in the book on Page 74.

5.5. What about a TEACHER?

Why is it that a teacher thinks that they have to teach all the time, and that they cannot coach sometimes? I remember working in a school in Aberdeen for a few days, and at the end when I was saying my farewells, a teacher said to me, "I wish I could teach my students the way that you do?"

This took me aback, and I said, "So, why don't you?" to which I was told that they have to stick to the curriculum and the way that they'd been told to teach.

For me, when a student asks me a question, I love asking them, "What do you think?", and they always have an answer. I am sure that there are teachers out there who do this, but there are too many who just give the students the answer first.

Take yourself back to when you first started to walk. It was you who decided when to walk, and which foot went forward first. Then when you fell over, it was you who got up and tried again. You were not told what to do or had someone holding each leg in turn. Or were you?

So, why don't teachers give the students a chance to answer their own question, because in my opinion, the majority know the answer, but the easy option is to get the teacher to give it to them.

If there are any teachers reading this book, then next time a student asks you a question, simply say to them, "What do you think?" When they give you an answer, then ask them, "What else?"

You will be surprised how many of the students will have a go at giving you the answer to their own question. The benefits to you, as the teacher, will include the fact that you are actually doing some coaching, and for the student, they will feel great that they are being allowed to use their own brain more often.

As Nike say, "Just Do It".

There will also be lots of situations in schools where the Headmaster needs to discuss situations with teachers, where a coaching approach would be the most appropriate. In a similar way, teachers talking to other teachers, either on a one-to-one basis or in meetings, could use the coaching approach to resolve issues.

CHAPTER 6

—

LEADING UP TO THE "TOOLBOX"

The first thing that you need to recognise is that whenever you are about to talk to anyone about an issue that they are facing, then, from my experience, **what they tell you is their issue is not necessarily the real issue**. It is at this stage that you need to be grateful that you are reading this particular book as it will help you to resolve this situation, in order to identify what the real issue is that needs to be addressed.

Also, a good coach should be non-judgemental, and therefore parents reading this book, who want to help their children resolve their issues, instead of arguing with them, will be able to use this toolbox, bearing this point in mind.

At the end of the day, **this book will help take the person with an issue (the client) from where they are today to where they want to be in the future**. The 'toolbox', and knowing how to use it, will ensure that this happens, resulting in a happy 'client' every time.

A question that I am asked prior to the coaching starting is, "How many sessions is this likely to take?" My answer to this is simply that I do not know, but it will take as many as is necessary to resolve the client's issue. In my seventeen years of coaching, I have resolved some issues in one session, while I had one client where it was over twenty sessions, as the goal post kept on changing.

By the way, when I talk about a coaching session, I am talking about one that lasts one hour. I do remember on one particular occasion where a mother wanted her daughter to have a trial one hour coaching session with me to see if it would appeal to her. I agreed to this request. However, I would not recommend this as a habit. In this particular case, I knew the mother, and she was spending money with me on another business I was running at that time.

On the day of the coaching session, I thought that it had gone really well, and at the end when I asked her when she would like the next session, she said that she didn't want one. I was absolutely flabbergasted. After a fifteen minute discussion, she said that she would like a three hour session and get everything discussed, after which she would know how to move forward with her life. Once more, I agreed to this request and the session took place one week later. It actually only lasted one and three quarter hours, after which she was one very satisfied client, who had thoroughly enjoyed the session. By the way, I was paid for the whole three hours that was booked. Always remember that time is money, and if you have allocated time to coach one person, this has stopped you from booking in another client.

I learned a lot from this episode, and am very willing to go along with **some** requests from a client, even it is not my norm.

CHAPTER 7

—

ERIC'S COACHING STYLE – THE 'TOOLBOX'

7.1. The WANT Tool

This is the first tool that I need to tell you about, because **I, personally, will only coach those people who WANT to be coached.** This might sound strange to some of you, but there are many parents out there who would love their children to have some coaching, but the child does not want to be coached.

It is therefore critical that, if you don't want to waste your time, then you must make it very clear to any parent up front that before you will coach their child, they need to talk to them about the coaching. In most cases, and totally understandable, children have no idea what coaching is. To help parents, I offer to send them some testimonials from previous child clients, so they can see what other children have said about the benefits of my coaching with them.

Case Studies

I had one situation where it was very clear that the daughter had agreed to the coaching to keep her parents happy, but she was just paying lip service to it, and during the sessions it was obvious that she was not interested. She was also not doing any of the homework being set by myself, based on the fact that she felt she knew it all. As you can imagine, the coaching finished much sooner than was necessary for the daughter to change. Ironically, this was one person who needed the coaching more than any other person I have ever coached. In this case, there was only one loser.

Ironically, when running a workshop recently on the subject of Coaching, I was challenged about **NEVER** coaching anyone who doesn't want to be coached. It really made me think, and took my mind back to when I had this situation, different to the one mentioned earlier, when a mother asked me if I'd give her daughter a one-off one hour coaching session to see what she thought.

I did this willingly, and during the session addressed a number of the issues that this girl was facing, and because she saw that there were solutions to them, she agreed to more coaching sessions, as we had not covered all of her issues. We had seven more coaching sessions, at the end of which, she was a different young lady and far more confident about herself.

So, keep an open mind if someone doesn't want to be coached, and see if there is another way before you decline to coach that person.

7.2. The 'Probing' tool

Coaching is all about helping someone, who has a real issue, that they will describe to you either in one word right through to a whole speech. You may hear phrases like *"I need a coach to help my confidence"*, *"I have a real issue going on at home that needs to be resolved"* or *"My son doesn't want to go to University, can you help please?"*

Whatever it is that you hear initially, it is imperative that you do not take this at face value, but realise that this is where your worth as a coach comes into play. The skill that you have in asking questions now comes to the fore, and you must now start using this 'probing tool' of yours to truly understand what the real issue is that you need to address.

Case Studies

Imagine receiving a phone call when the person at the other end states that they have been given your name, and then says, *"I am going through a horrendous divorce and I need your help".*

As the coach, you need to know in more detail just what the potential client means by stating 'a horrendous divorce'. Out comes 'the probing tool', and you ask, *"Could you please tell me more about why you call it a horrendous divorce?"*

Other key facts then come to light that make one realise the divorce proceedings have been going on for a few years and the client's friends have been advising her to make sure that she gets as much money as she can from her husband, whereas **the real reason why she has phoned you is that she actually just wants her life back again.**

WOW!! So, the 'probing tool' is key at an early stage in order to identify what the real issue is, and not what the coach might have assumed it is, based on the initial words used by the potential client.

I also recall coaching a woman who said that she needed coaching as she wanted to be more confident and more assertive. As you can imagine this needs to become much more specific from the client, and so the 'probing tool' of the coach is the one that has to be used immediately.

This is where the coach really shows their skill in asking some key questions to elicit **when** the client wants to be both more confident and more assertive. You might even want to use your 'probing tool' to ascertain a lot more about situations for the client when the two words of 'confidence' and 'assertive' crop up.

This is why you need a toolbox, because the client is telling you what they believe is their problem, but your role is to put their words into the words that will ultimately help you to find a solution for them. The end result: One happy client.

So don't be afraid to Probe, probe and probe even more.

In actual fact, I realised something else the other day when coaching someone for the first time, and she was telling me why she felt she needed a coach. I listened intently to what she had to say, **and then realised that I had to think on my feet** as to what I was going to say, in response to what I had heard.

Thinking about this situation later on that day, a number of thoughts occurred to me. Firstly, what I had said to her was based on my years of coaching experience, and would be different to what another coach would have said. It also made me draw the analogy, with my football background, of how a referee feels when he/she blows their whistle and makes a decision on the spur of the moment, based on what they have seen.

However, the key difference is that with football, and all the cameras observing the match, the referee's decision will be scrutinised over and over by the so called pundits, plus with the latest technology of VAR (Video Assistant Referee).

This will not be the case with the coach. So, make **YOUR** decision based on what you have heard from the client, and ask what you need to ask, in order to probe into what the client is telling you and you can fully understand how you can help them.

In the case of the coach or the referee, a decision had to be made, that eventually could have been the right one, but also could have been the wrong one. The important thing is that a decision was made.

Who would want to be a referee versus who would want to be a coach?

7.3. The 'Marks Out Of Ten' tool

Following on from the 'probing' tool, this next tool can be used alongside. This will help clarify precisely why the client needs you as their coach. This is critical. It could be as simple as *"I am not a confident person, and I need to have confidence for my future"*. In order for you, the coach, to gauge how serious this issue is, I would ask, "So, on a ten point scale, where 1 is *I do not have any confidence whatsoever*, and 10 is *I am the most confident person you'll meet in this whole world*, what would you score yourself currently?"

The client might respond, *"I would say that I'm a 6"*. At this point, the coach then knows how serious a problem they are going to have to address. This is a great starting point. Just to put the importance of this tool into context, I have had one client who scored themselves a -2. From a coach's perspective, this will either worry you, or as it was for me, a wonderful challenge to help my client truly change their life. If you are asking yourself how I got on, then it took quite a number of coaching sessions, but the client leads a great life now. The Power of Coaching.

If the coach does not use this particular tool initially, then they are just addressing the issue itself <u>with no regard to the extent of the problem</u>.

As the coach, I would then ask, *"So what mark out of 10 would you love to be scoring, where a 10 is I am the most confident person you'll meet in this whole world?"* The answer that I have been given in the majority of cases has been a 9 or 10.

However, a number of clients have stopped short and scored an 8. Why? Because they feel that if they said a 9 or 10 then they would be perceived as either Cocky or Arrogant. This is their belief and I would not even try to change their mind, but simply get on with making them feel more confident.

I cannot stress enough how powerful, and necessary it is to use this 1 to 10 scale, especially after having heard the client explain to you what they believe is the issue that they want you to help them resolve.

You are now in the position where you not only know what your starting point is, but also where your end point is that will satisfy your client.

Depending on what the client tells you is their issue, then you can use the ten point scale on various topics. A few that I have used include Confidence, Life in General, Happiness and Enthusiasm for the job (this was coaching a teacher). Depending on who you end up getting as your clients, and what their problems are, you can use your imagination to find another ten point scale to use.

Case Studies

I remember coaching a young lady who had just completed her first year at University, and had come back home with lots of issues that needed addressing before she returned to University for the start of her second year.

In this instance, I got her to give me scores on "Life at University", "Life in general" and "Her confidence".

For 'Life at University' she scored herself currently at a 3 but wanted to be scoring a 9 by the time she returned to University. For 'Life in General' she scored herself currently at 6 but wanted to be a 9 by the time she returned to University. Finally, she scored herself a 5 on her current level of confidence, and wanting to be a 10 going into her second year at University.

As you can imagine, when you are given scores like this, you can see the power of the "marks out of 10 tool". Immediately, you are able to move on to some of the other tools, knowing that any increase to her current scores is going to motivate her to do even more to achieve the scores that she truly wants.

This then moves you on nicely and logically to the next tool in your "toolbox".

7.4. The 'Timing' Tool

So, with the 'confidence' client, you know that their level of confidence is currently scoring a 5, and that they would ideally like to be scoring a 9 or 10. What you are not aware of is how long they have been scoring a 5, but as a coach, you are more concerned with moving them forward to reach their goal of scoring a 9 or 10.

So, you **ask them for a date** when they would like to be scoring their 9 or 10. What I have found is that the majority of clients will give you a date in about nine months time, because their belief is that it will take time before they can have the confidence that they truly desire.

On the assumption that I will be coaching the client on a weekly basis, for one hour coaching sessions at a time, I ask them, "How would you like it if you will be scoring your confidence a 9 or 10 in two months time, or even less?"

Of course, they say that would be wonderful, and I immediately tell them that is my personal goal to get them there in that period of time.

Why do I use this approach? Quite simply, I have observed companies taking on projects that have far longer completion times than are actually needed. I have observed people working out in gyms, setting themselves goals that are easily achieved, but not challenging. Why not just take a look at politics and how long is put aside to tackle key issues? Shorter time frames encourage a greater motivation and enthusiasm to reach the end goal.

This whole issue of timing is even more critical at this point in time, early April 2018, when there have been nearly 50 killings in the UK so far in 2018. All I hear is that we are tackling the problem, with solutions about educating children in schools, talking to local communities, etc. What I am never hearing is what is going to be done TODAY to tackle the problem. How many more killings will there be this month of April 2018? It will not be zero.

There are solutions when there is a will to find them, regardless of the cost. The Government needs to set themselves a target of reducing the number of killings to zero within a month, and then with this goal, ideas will be forthcoming. Unfortunately, we never hear about timings, and so the killings go on.

So, enough of my ranting, and back to my book, and the 'Timing tool'.

From my experience over the years, **setting smaller time periods always results in achieving goals that the clients are thrilled with**.

For me, I personally want to see the client get to where they want to get to AS SOON AS POSSIBLE.

Case Studies

Very recently, I had a client who had a real confidence issue and wanted to achieve a 10 from a starting point of 5. When we met one week after his first one hour coaching session, he had taken all the actions we'd discussed at the first session, and now scored himself an 8. When we had finished his second one hour coaching session, he felt like he was a 9.5. I still see that client and he is a totally different person to when I first met him. I sincerely hope that you can help clients change as quickly as I did with this particular client.

Earlier on we spoke about only coaching someone who WANTS to be coached. This client most certainly did and hopefully, you will find similar clients who will make you feel absolutely wonderful, and know that you have made a true impact on your client's life.

Another client I coached had lots of issues that had arisen from her early life and I could understand very clearly why she scored herself a 5 on the confidence scale. Working with her, using some of the tools to follow, I could not believe the person who walked into a subsequent coaching session, one month later. The way she walked in, and the smile on her face, told me that she had been working very hard on what we'd discussed. My first question to her was, "So where on the ten point scale of confidence do you put yourself right now?" Yes, you've guessed it – a 10.

7.5. Summary at this stage

So far we have spoken about four key tools. Can you remember and name them?

If you said **"The WANT" Tool, "The Probing Tool", "The Marks Out Of Ten Tool" and "The Timing Tool"**, then you are obviously taking on board some initial tools that will help you help others.

It does not matter what the issue is, I personally will use all of these four tools every time. Why? You must clarify up front that the person to be coached DOES actually want to be coached. If this is the case, then you can proceed to determine precisely what the issue is that the coachee really wants a solution to, and that is not necessarily what they have initially told you. This is where you will find out how good you are at asking key open questions to get the coachee talking to you in sentences and not just giving you Yes/No answers.

It is also critical that you know how big, or small, the issue is, and this is where the 'Marks Out Of Ten' tool is very powerful. In the past, as I stated earlier in this book, **I had someone scoring a**

-2 on how they viewed their life at that point in time. You then know that they have come to see, or talk to you for a very real reason.

Again it is critical to know how long they are prepared to wait until they get a solution to their issue. It is up to you, but from my perspective, I always want to get a solution for them much quicker than the date they give me. However, this will be up to you to decide, in conjunction with a discussion with your client.

7.6. The 'Negative Issues' Tool

From what we have discussed so far, you can see that my coaching style uses a simple process that flows. Think about any good franchise, and you will see that they use a process that any new employee can look at and follow. So, with McDonalds, it does not matter which branch you visit, anywhere in the world, you should get the same service and product, provided that their process that is laid down, is followed.

So it is with 'the Eric Gilston coaching process'.

You now have clarified what the real issue is, you know the extent of the issue and you know when the coachee would like it resolved.

Now it is the time to determine what needs to be done to move them forward to a higher score out of 10.

Case Studies

Let's look at a situation that I have had to deal with on numerous occasions, viz. where a teenager is lacking confidence. In this case, I ask for a list of occasions when the coachee feels confident. **I always start with the positives** going on in the client's life as this is something that the client will want to talk about, rather than the negatives going on in their lives.

The list tends to include, "when I'm with my family", "when I'm with my friends", "when I'm listening to my music" plus some other things that are personal to them.

We now move on to asking the question, "So tell me the occasions when you are **not** confident?"

Listen very carefully to what the coachee is telling you, and ask questions if you are not 100% sure about what they are saying on any point. The list is usually quite extensive, **so listen without making any judgemental comments.** Things that have been said include, "when I meet new people", "when I have to make a presentation", "when I'm asked questions in class", "when I get certain text messages or emails". The list is endless.

I would recommend that when the coachee is telling you about these occasions, that **you write them all down**, as opposed to trying to remember them in your head. You just do not know how many things they are going to mention.

There will be some coachees who will give you a very comprehensive list without any prompting, but there will be others where you will need to draw out occasions when they are not confident. You can do this very simply by asking "and what else?" and then keeping silent to allow their thought process to engage.

Your role then is to work with the coachee to find solutions to each of those occasions when they are telling you that they are not confident.

Let's work through one of those occasions. Assume that you are coaching a teenager:-

Coach: So you have said that you are not confident when you meet new people. Can you give me an example of when this happened recently?

Coachee: I went out with some of my close friends and they brought some of their friends along. However, I didn't talk to any of them as I was not confident to do so.

Coach: What did you think was the worst thing that would have happened if you had spoken to one of them?

Coachee: They would have ignored me and not wanted to speak to me.

Coach: Did you see any of them do that with any of your close friends?

Coachee: No.

Coach: So, what makes you think that they would have done that, but only to you?

Coachee: Don't really know.

Coach: Can I make a suggestion?

Coachee: Yes please.

Coach: Next time that you are in company with people that you do not know, be confident enough to go up to someone and introduce yourself by saying, "Hi, my name is Melissa, what's yours?" They might reply with "Hi Melissa, my name is Alexandra". You can then quickly jump in and say something appropriate to where you are, e.g. "Lovely to meet you Alexandra. So, who do you know here?"

What you have done is got the other person to talk first, as people love to talk about themselves, while you are just listening. Alexandra might then ask you something, by which time you are confident enough to reply, and a new friend has been made.

In my role as the coach, I then ask when the coachee will next be meeting some new people, and challenge them to talk to at least two new people using this approach. I then ask them if they are willing to do that. In every case in the past, the coachee has accepted the challenge, been successful and grown in confidence. This, in turn, has reduced the number of occasions when your client was not confident, and you can move on to help the client with the next occasion when they said they were not confident.

7.7. The 'Ranking' Tool

So, going back to when your client has given you all the occasions when they do not feel confident, and they cannot think of any more, I would then read back to them the list of what they have told me are all those occasions when they are not confident. As I want them to get their confidence back as quickly as possible, I ask them to rank their items on the list in order of importance to them.

Case Studies

I recall coaching one teenager who had told me that she was not confident "when she was in the company of other teenagers who she did not know", "when she was asked questions in class by the teachers" and "when she was going into exams".

I asked her to rank these three occasions in order of importance to her for getting solutions to each. She ranked "when I'm asked questions in class" as her Number 1, then "when she was going into exams as Number 2.

I then asked her, *"Why are you not confident when you're asked questions in class?"* Her response was, *"I'm worried in case I give the wrong answer and the rest of the class laugh at me"*. I then said to her, *"So when other people answer questions in class, does everyone laugh at them?"* The response was, *"No, never"*.

This fact is quite an interesting one in situations when people say that they are not confident. Why do I say that it is 'interesting'? Well, people have a choice, in certain situations, of being confident or not confident. Yet, it would appear that **the option that is chosen is one that they believe only applies to them.**

I followed up her answer by asking, *"So, next time you are asked a question in class, would you be prepared to answer the teacher's question?"* The answer was a spontaneous *"Yes".*

As your goal as the coach is to make the coachee more confident, I then asked, *"How would you feel if your answer to the question is the right one?"* The answer was, *"I would feel absolutely wonderful and pleased that I answered the question".*

I then went on to say, *"On that basis, will you start answering more questions from now on?"* Of course, I then got a Yes response.

To keep the momentum going, I then asked, *"So what do you think this will do to your confidence?"* Again, the answer was, "It will improve".

You can then go on to use the same approach with the concern that the coachee has ranked as Number 2. By the time you have gone through all their concerns, in rank order, and by working together, come up with solutions to each concern that the coachee is very happy with, you are in a position to ask the coachee whether their score for confidence has increased.

Don't be too concerned if they say it hasn't, as they most likely will want to put everything you've gone through into practice. Then, and only then, will they be able to talk about their new score on Confidence. So, make a note that you will ask about their confidence level at the start of the next coaching session. Also, ask about the occasions that they put into practice what you had coached, and ask about their feelings at the time.

7.8. The 'One-Liner' Tool

There are times during a coaching session where a one-liner is appropriate, and so as a coach I find it very useful to have a few in my vocabulary. I have therefore included later on in this book over fifty of my favourites.

Case Studies

The one that I use the most ties up with my coachees using negative language. Let me give you some examples. *"I should improve my confidence"*, *"I will try and do this by next week"*. It is at this point when these sentences are being quoted that I say to them **"Change begins with language".**

I then ask them to rephrase what they have just said, but state it as a confident person would. You will then get the alternatives of *"I will improve my confidence"* and *"I will do this by next week".*

The best story that I have for you was when I was coaching someone who had mentioned to me at the previous session that her dad was going to buy a business, and so I asked her if it had happened. She said that in a conversation with her dad, she'd asked him if it had happened, and he replied, "I'm not sure, but I might buy it". To which, his daughter said *"Dad, change begins with language"*. He then said, "It's that Eric again. O.K. I will buy the company". **The power of one-liners.**

I would say that the one-liner that I use the second most in coaching sessions is **"If it's to be, it's up to me".** Why? Quite simply because when people need a coach, it is usually due to the fact that the client has not been able to resolve their issue on their own, and have looked to blame other people for their current situation. So, at some point in the coaching session, they realise that it is up to them to change the situation. Hence, **"If it's to be, it's up to me"**.

7.9. The 'My Experience' Tool

There will be occasions when the coaching session is progressing very nicely when, you as the coach realise that you have a story, from your own experience in life that is most appropriate to be told at that moment to get your point across.

Case Studies

I had a situation coaching a young girl of 17, who was a singer, but was not confident when she messed up and sang a wrong note. I drew an analogy for her, relaying the story of a young rugby player who I coached, who found that every time he messed up a pass or dropped the ball when given a pass, it would be on his mind for the rest of the game.

In both instances, I pointed out that once the messing up had happened, there was no turning back to correct the error. Instead, both of them needed to forget what had happened immediately and focus on respectively the rest of the song and the rest of the game of rugby.

I then checked with both of them if that made sense, and that they would do that the next time an error happened? They both agreed.

I have also used in this situation, an experience that I'm sure some of you would have gone through in your life when driving. You go past a speed camera and are convinced that it flashed and you will be receiving a letter in the post telling you about your subsequent fine and loss of points. So, for the next two weeks you worry about this letter, and guess what – it never arrives.

The moral of this story is that once the event has happened, it has happened, you cannot turn the clock back, so move forward with your life, your song, your game of rugby.

In this situation, you are not using a story, to tell the client what to do, but simply using it to get a point across in order to help them work out the solution to that particular situation.

The great thing about this particular tool is that we have all had different experiences in life, and talking about a relevant one to the issue that your client is mentioning, will help the client see it from a different perspective. It should be noted that the experience does not have to have come from a coaching session, but simply a similar experience in your lifetime.

7.10. The 'Anchor' Tool

Sometimes when running a coaching session, you could find yourself with a coachee who is lacking confidence in being able to do a certain thing, but you, as the coach, know that the coachee has done something similar in the past, or you believe that they might recall an occasion when they were totally capable of doing what their 'mindset' told them they can't.

It is at times like this that the coach needs to apply the 'Anchor' tool from their toolbox.

Case Studies

Here is an example of when I applied it, very successfully. I was coaching an extremely talented female singer, who was booked to perform in an auditorium with an audience of four hundred people. Her mindset was telling her that she would just crumble as soon as she got on stage and looked out to the large audience.

So, I asked her to think of an occasion when she had felt really confident and had performed at the top of her game. She could not recall an occasion in front of a live audience, but recalled a recent occasion when in the shower.

I got her to get a clear picture of herself, repeating that performance, singing and hitting new notes, and really feeling great. I then asked her to think of a word to associate with that great performance. She chose POTENTIAL. Don't ask me why, as I did not pursue the reason for this word.

I then told her that this word would become her anchor, and that every time she said the word Potential, her mind would immediately switch to seeing, and hearing herself performing her song as she did in the shower, and that would switch her mindset to feeling great about herself.

The power of this technique would mean that when she needed to perform in front of four hundred people, her mindset would take her to a higher starting point than if she was just starting from scratch, and a low point of not feeling confident.

Quite naturally, she was sceptical about using this technique, but was very willing to give it a go, as the converse was not being able to perform in front of a large audience. Suffice to say, that when the performance took place, she was a huge success, and now looks forward to performing in front of any size audience.

This is a very powerful technique, and when you get the chance to apply it, use it and see both the impact it will have on you and your clients.

Simply remember that when you get your client to think of a time when they were doing something really well, and feeling good about themselves, you get them to visualise the occasion, where they were, how they felt and get them to verbalise it all to you. Watch their facial expressions as they tell you, and then ask them for the word that they had chosen as their anchor.

7.11. The 'Mindset' Tool

The mind is very powerful, but we all have choices as to how we let it affect our lives. If you want to cry, you can let your mind work its power, and you will cry.

In a similar way, the majority of my clients need my help because they have allowed their minds to think negatively about things going on in their lives. The longer that they have allowed this to happen, the worse their situation had become.

My goal is very simple and straightforward, and that is to change their mindset to that of thinking positively about their situation. Let me give you one key example of where I have done this.

Case Studies

I had a client who was very conscious about having acne, and how he perceived himself. This was severely affecting his confidence and was stressing him out.

I started off by asking him how many of his friends, or non-friends, had ever commented about the spots on his face. At most, he said about 10%. So, I said that if 90% were not making any comment, what could he do in the future about the 10% who chose to make a comment.

He said that he could rise above their comments and just ignore them. I then asked him what the benefits would be to him if he took this action. He said that this would definitely reduce the stress that he was putting himself under. The conversation then went on to choices, and my client realised that he had to change some of the choices that he was making in his life. He also realised that he had to stop his mind making assumptions about how people perceived him. So, his thought that they were looking at him and thinking about his spots and acne could be totally false, and actually their judgement of him was a positive one because they liked him for who he was.

What I had done was not 'rocket science' but just by asking some key questions, my client soon realised that he had been the cause of making his life miserable to that point, and that he was in total charge of making a key change to his life, by adopting a positive, and not a negative mindset.

"If it's to be, it's up to me".

Having seen him a few months later, he walks around totally confident about himself, and leads a new life.

This 'Mindset' tool was written on the morning of the 1st November 2017. You might be wondering why I should be mentioning this particular date. Well later that day, while reading the Evening Standard, I saw a headline that read, "The final step for Spurs to join elite is all in the mind, insists Pochettino."

For those of you not interested in football, I do apologise, but I felt it was necessary to include this in my book for a number of reasons, viz.

- Here was a football manager (Spurs Manager) recognising the important role the mind plays with footballers.
- Spurs were playing that evening against the current holders of the Champions League – Real Madrid.
- I have always supported Spurs

The article itself quoted, "Mauricio Pochettino believes the final hurdle his Tottenham team must overcome is a mental one; establishing the self-belief to compete and thrive at the highest level".

So, this just goes to show the power of the mind, and how its importance plays a role not only in everyone's daily life, but also extends to professional footballers, and the difference between being an ordinary team as opposed to an excellent one.

To conclude this section on the Mindset, Spurs obviously responded to their Manager's viewpoint, and won the match 3-1, proving that you do not win games just by having great players with great skills, but on the day, your mindset will play a key role. The Manager added "We are able to compete with teams now on a physical and mental level".

So the choice is yours. If you want to think negatively about your current situation, then that is up to you. However, the benefits to you, by simply changing your mindset to that of a positive person, are immense.

As Nike say, "Just do it".

7.12. The 'Benefits' Tool

There are times during a coaching session when a coachee has come up with a number of answers to a question posed by the coach. However, to help the coachee in making a decision as to which is the best answer, I find that by asking the simple question "What will be the benefits to you?", or something similar, then clarification becomes the order of the day. Let me give you some examples.

Case Studies

I was coaching a senior manager in a company and we were talking about how that person was perceived in the company, and we had not only discussed many aspects to that question, but also what could be done to change the perception.

At this point, I could see that the client had enjoyed this approach to looking at the issue, and so to move it forward to get the thinking around the actions to be taken, I took each of the points that had been identified as to what could be done to change the perception, and asked "So, what would be the benefits if you did this?"

Four responses came out very quickly, with a smile on the client's face, and we quickly moved on to the actions that needed to be taken.

Another good example of asking about 'The Benefits', is when you are coaching young people. If you can get them thinking about the benefits of them taking action, then they are far more likely to do it. Here is an example.

This one was when I was coaching a teenager who had fallen behind on handing in their homework on time. So, I posed the question, "What would be the benefits to you of doing every piece of homework on the day that it is given to you, even if it doesn't have to be handed in for a week?"

Spontaneously, I received answers that included, "I will not be panicking the night before a homework is due in", "I will have more time to speak to my friends on the phone", "I will not get hassle from the teachers at school", and many more.

The client could see that these benefits would be most beneficial, and therefore a change to the mindset whenever homework was handed out had to be initiated immediately.

Another good example of when I used this Benefits tool was when coaching a student who was forever late in arriving at school in the mornings. He had all the excuses for why he was late, but when I asked him what the benefits would be to him for arriving early at school, he was very forthcoming.

"I would be relaxed before my first lesson", "I could talk to my friends about any outstanding homework", "My teachers would look at me in a different light". These were just three of his spontaneous Benefits that he could think of.

So, I asked him whether he thought that these benefits were worth going for, and he agreed. The next discussion was around the excuses that he had made for why he was always late, and whether he could think of what he needed to do to change these from happening.

Of course, he had the solutions, and agreed to put them in place the next day. It is now two months later since we had that coaching session, and he is now in early EVERY day, and reaping lots of new benefits as well as those he'd identified initially.

7.13. The 'Mentoring while Coaching' Tool

Earlier on in this book, I gave you what I consider to be the best definition of Coaching, viz. ***Coaching is not a prescription with set answers for every situation. It is about encouraging your client to expand on their thoughts and feelings and, in so doing, they will develop their own strategies for dealing with a given issue. You are there to help in this process and then to help them evolve their own tactics and actions that will bring those strategies into reality. Once evolved, you will keep a supportive pressure on to ensure that the actions are taken.***

Over the 17 years of coaching, I have realised that there are times when a coaching session cannot just be 100% coaching, and applying the aforementioned definition of coaching. Hence why I am including this tool in my toolbox so that any of you reading this book, and finding that you are mentoring while carrying out a coaching session, should not feel guilty in any shape or form.

Case Studies

Let me give you some examples that have happened to me, especially when coaching teenagers.

A coaching session has gone really well where I have worked with the coachee to address their issues, and they are happy with the strategies that they have to take to move them forward. However, I realise that they have never set goals for themselves in the past, and that teaching them a technique like SMART would be advantageous to them, not only for the present but for the rest of their lives.

I can now change my Coaching hat to that of the Mentor's hat, as I can mentor them on the way that SMART works. However, within the explaining, I can still employ some coaching by asking questions and doing a lot of listening to what they have to say.

Does that make sense to you as to why we must have the 'Mentoring while Coaching' tool in our toolbox?

For all of you reading this book, then you must recognise that you will have some expertise that your coachee does not have, and could be useful to impart to the coachee, if and only if, it is relevant to the issue(s) being faced by the coachee.

So, another example of where I have done some mentoring within a coaching session with a teenager, was when we were talking about the stress that they were encountering in numerous situations, one of which was when studying for exams and not being able to remember facts and key dates.

As I have some key techniques, that I teach both young people and adults, on how to remember facts, numbers and names of people, then I was able to incorporate these techniques into the coaching session.

So, pulling all of this together, a coaching session is one that relates to the definition given above. However, **if all you are doing is teaching your client/coachee information where you consider yourself to be an expert, then you are taking on the role of being a mentor, and you are not running a coaching session.**

I suppose this lays open the possibility for someone to write a book titled "The Mentors Toolbox". Do you think that is you? If it is not you, then you could find that this will be one of MY next books. Watch this space.

7.14 The 'Affirmations' Tool

Have you ever heard the term 'affirmation'? Not all of you, so let me explain it as I do when coaching. I say that affirmations are statements that bring the future to the present, and must satisfy three criteria, viz. they must be Positive, Present Tense and Personal. Affirmations help you overcome negative thoughts and help you visualize who you want to be.

Case Studies

Earlier on this book, I mentioned coaching a rower wanting to get into the GB squad. Well part of his coaching was to get him to put together a couple of affirmations, and this is what he came up with. *"I know that I am a fantastic rower who deserves to be part of the GB squad." "I work extremely hard at training to ensure that I retain my place in the GB squad".*

In order for him to become this person, I told him to put these statements into his phone and also to put them into a Word document in capital letters. Also, in order to get them into his subconscious, I told him to read the two affirmations last thing at night and first thing in the morning.

The more he would look at the affirmations, the quicker he would believe he was this person and start to behave like someone who was actually in the GB rowing squad.

I have used affirmations in numerous coaching sessions and they are truly powerful. For the cricketer that I coached, she put together affirmations about what she wanted to achieve at every practice session with the England squad, and by doing this, she exceeded what she'd written in her affirmations – every time. She would read her affirmations before going out onto the field of play, and then become that person.

Other situations where I have used affirmations in coaching include a young lady who was not very confident, and in school got very anxious about speaking her mind for fear of what others in the class might say.

We spoke about affirmations and she came up with, *"I am an extremely confident person who can speak their mind freely without being anxious".* She then went ahead with using her computer to put this in big capital letters on an A4 sheet of paper, read it to herself every night before going to bed, than again first thing in the morning and then on the way to school.

Within a day, she started to speak her mind in class, and found that it wasn't as bad as she thought it would be. With this, she started to do it more & more, her confidence grew and her anxiety disappeared.

Another student that I was coaching was studying doing a film & TV course, and was not only passionate about making films but being the best. We agreed that an affirmation describing how he wanted to be in the future would help him behave like that person now. He came up with *"I am passionately motivated to make great films for the next generation of films, and as I am confident, I am meeting people who can make like minded films".* Wow!!! I will be monitoring this student's name in the future, as I believe he will be a big name in the film industry.

7.15. The 'Empathy' Tool

Earlier on this book, I mentioned the importance of being a good listener, in order to be a good coach.

Over the years, I have found it so important, during that first five minutes, to really get to know the person that you are about to coach, and to show empathy with what they are telling you.

It is critical that you avoid using the phrase *"I know how you feel"*, as we all feel differently about the same issue. The temptation will be there, but please do not say it. It's similar to how we love interrupting someone when they are talking to you, because "you know what they are going to say". No, you don't. So, next time, just let them finish talking, as difficult as it might be.

The reason that someone needs a coach, is that they have a real issue that they need resolved. Therefore, **the first step is someone showing some empathy and just listening to them. Hence, the non-judgemental coach.**

You will also find during the coaching session, the coachee says something that requires you to allow them time and space just to talk. However long this takes, allow it to happen, with you saying things occasionally like "yes", "um", etc. Whatever you might want to say, save it until the coachee finishes, even if there is some silence while they are thinking. Watching them carefully will tell you when you can say something.

Case Studies

I remember one instance when I was coaching someone who was to have a mediation meeting to agree with her husband a few points about their children's welfare. As you can imagine, the wife had a number of concerns about all the possible "what- ifs", and so it was critical before I went into a coaching mode, that I allowed her to get everything off her chest and, for me to just listen.

I also recall another instance where I was doing some coaching over the telephone, and needing to listen to a woman explaining to me a lot of facts about how her husband had treated her over a period of four years. In view of the fact that I was giving her the space to talk, with my occasional 'really' or 'yes', she suddenly stopped her story and said, " Are you still there Eric?". To which I replied, "Yes, I am just listening". She then blew me away, when she said, "I was worried, because no one has ever allowed me to speak for that long without interrupting me". That's showing empathy.

CHAPTER 8

—

A FULL COACHING SESSION

In view of the fact that I have just shown you 14 tools that I use, in various permutations and computations, I thought that you might find it very useful if I actually demonstrate to you a complete REAL coaching session that actually took place, and has been briefly mentioned in section 7.11. The Mindset Tool.

A little background for you is that I am coaching individuals at a school and am given minimal information about why a person has been sent to see me. I therefore start the session by establishing a rapport and asking the student why they believe that they are seeing me.

In this instance, the student told me that his acne was affecting how he perceived himself. I asked him what impact this was having on his life, to which he said that he was getting extremely stressed with it. **(The Probing Tool)** This led me quite easily to ask him how he scored himself on a ten point scale of confidence. He gave me a score of 5 and said that he wanted to be a 10 by the end of May 2017. **(The Marks Out Of Ten Tool, and The Timing Tool)** This immediately told me the importance of this issue for this particular student, as this first session was on the 19th May 2017.

We then spoke about the benefits to him when he was scoring a 10 by the end of May. He said that he would be happy, not stressing, not worrying, feeling good because he was looking good, and he would be more positive about life in general.**(The Benefits Tool)**

I then asked him to tell me all the occasions when he was confident. Included in his list were being with friends, being with family and making creative music. I then went on to asking him about the times when he was not confident, as I knew that if I could help him overcome these occasions, he would be on his way to scoring a 10 on confidence. **(The Negative Issues Tool)**

He mentioned three things, and I then got him to rank them in the order for which he wanted a resolution. **(The Ranking Tool)** Number One was Stress, and the things that play on his mind. What was very interesting at this point was when I asked him to name when the occasions were that he had most stress. My expectation was that he would mention solely the spots on his face, but in actual fact that he mentioned two other things that were going on in his life that were giving him a lot of stress.

So, again I had the opportunity to use the Ranking tool, and I got him to rank the three things giving him stress, in the order he wanted to get resolutions. First and foremost was the stress from the spots, and so I asked him to tell me why this was giving him stress. **(The Empathy Tool)** He spoke about how he felt that people were judging him, and he felt very strongly about this.

I started off by asking him how many of his friends, or non-friends, had ever commented about the spots on his face. At most, he said about 10%. So, I said that if 90% were not making any comment, what could he do in the future about the 10% who chose to make a comment.

He said that he could rise above their comments and just ignore them. I then asked him what the benefits would be to him if he took this action. He said that this would definitely reduce the stress that he was putting himself under. The conversation then went on to choices, and my client realised that he had to change some of the choices that he was making in his life. I quoted to him, "If you want to change something in your life, you have to change something in your life". **(The One Liner Tool)**

He also realised that he had to stop his mind making assumptions about how people perceived him, as he had absolutely no proof of this. So, his thought that they were looking at him, and thinking about his spots and acne, could be totally false, and actually **their judgement of him was a positive one because they liked him for who he was.**

I then quoted to him another of my one-liners, viz. If it's to be, it's up to me. He then realised that he was the cause of his stress, and not other people.

Without going through the other things causing stress to my client, suffice to say that he was scoring a 10 by the end of May, and to this day, he is one of the most confident people you could ever meet. The coaching sessions were a turning point in his life, and in my opinion, this client will have a great future, and could even become an excellent life coach.

CHAPTER 9

—

FUTURE OPPORTUNITIES

9.1. Sport

At this stage in my coaching career, and with the numerous successes that I have had in changing clients' lives, I am not stopping, and have many more challenges that I would love to tackle.

As a qualified football coach and referee, there are many occasions when I see both Players and Managers going through a sticky patch, and things not going quite right. I would love to have the opportunity to go into a club and **coach these people to get their mindset changed**. I would even go so far as to say that I would not charge an initial fee, but get paid on agreed changes laid down before the coaching begins. Who wants to be the first club to give this a go?

This does not have to just apply to football. It could be a tennis player, a golfer, a rugby player, a cricketer and many more sports people.

I am so confident about my ability to create change in people's mindset that I would love to work with any football club or country that could be involved in a penalty shoot out. How many times have we seen players involved with their club, when they do not get promoted in play-offs, or playing for their country when they do not get through to the next round in a tournament, or they lose in a Cup Final? Let me coach that team prior to the possible shoot out. What have you got to lose, apart from your pride, your fans hurt, and much more? Give me a call nearer the time.

9.2. Schools

The opportunities here are endless. There is a real difference between teaching and coaching. I remember being at a school in Scotland, and having finished coaching there, a particular teacher having seen the impact that I'd had on her students said, "I wish I could do the things that you do". This really surprised me since she could use my approach of asking the students for their answers to questions being posed, compared to the teachers spontaneously giving the students the answers.

Just think back to when we were all young children and starting to walk. Correct me if I'm wrong, but I believe that as children **we** decide when we are going to walk and take our first steps without total instruction from our parents. Similarly when you see young children talking to each other, or children talking to their parents, they are not talking from scripts, it just comes out of their mouths and brains.

So, the young people of today have so much in their brains that we need to allow that to come out, rather than us assuming that we need to give them the answers before they have a chance to say what they think.

Therefore, at inset days, I would like to see a lot more schools getting coaches come in and run workshops to show the teachers how this can be done. I have a workshop all ready for the first schools to contact me, and the benefits for those students from a new way of teaching that incorporates coaching will be there for all the parents to see.

CHAPTER 10

—

TESTIMONIALS FOR ERIC GILSTON

In this chapter, I wanted to provide you with several genuine testimonials I have received from clients over the years. I believe that, by reading these, it will fill you with even more confidence that my coaching methods, techniques and tools *really* do work!

"When I first called Eric Gilston I assumed my life was in order and was in need of just a little bit of tweaking. But, after one session I came to realise that I had actually lost direction and belief in myself.

He gave me belief in everything I did and all that I will become. Most importantly, he made me believe in myself again and to translate change into a challenge and not an obstacle."

"May I say that the coaching you gave my 11 year old daughter when she had to make her Head Girl's speech to an audience of about 300 people absolutely transformed her presentation."

"I have no hesitation in recommending Eric to coach people who need to increase their confidence and self-belief and who want to gain or improve speaking skills. He will help anyone improve their personal and professional lives."

"Eric's coaching skills have helped me on numerous occasions when I needed a sounding board and confidante to clarify some key business decisions, and ensure that all the what if's had been covered."

"Thank you so much for all your help, encouragement and advice. I am sure X will continue to see you over the coming year and I am so pleased he has an independent person whose judgement I trust,

to help him move forward in his life and career choices. Thank you so much."

"My daughter thoroughly enjoyed her coaching sessions with Eric and gained a great deal. Even though I thought she was already quite a self-assured and able individual she is now much more confident in her abilities and is more able to present herself to others. She can focus her mind on what she wants to achieve and how to do it! The life skills learned are invaluable and Eric truly has the ability to focus in on a student's abilities and build on them."

"To whom it may concern

Eric came to work with our son Y, to coach and help him appreciate his attributes and to improve his self demeanour and confidence.

Over a series of sessions Eric managed to build a bond with Y and ascertained what was important and what was to be his guiding focus for his future.

Eric and Y sat together alone, for a number of sessions, with each session lasting 1 and half hours. Obviously as the sessions were confidential, we were not able to interfere with the content. However during the period of sessions and subsequent to the sessions, we have noticed a significant improvement in Y.

Not only is Y more confident in his spoken word, he seems more confident generally, carries himself in a tall and correct manner and is determined in his attitude.

Moreover during this period, X returned from school with a glowing school report and made the starting line up for the A team for Esher U12 Rugby .

Our son is a changed person and for this we must thank Eric and his coaching sessions. We have seen at first hand the benefits this can bring to Children and

we would not have a hesitation in recommending him to others and indeed plan to engage Eric's services for Y later in the year and for our daughter.

Thank you Eric"

From a school teacher:-

"Thank you so much Eric. A wonderful, inspirational, constructive and skill building experience. I would say that all of my 12 students have increased confidence levels and motivation".

From a Deputy Head:

"I just wanted to write to thank you for doing such a fantastic job with the students this week. Once again I was blown away with what they had produced and I really think it is a tremendously valuable programme. I know, however, that without your wise counsel the students would not be able to produce anything like the same result. They clearly loved working with you and I know a couple of them even went out to buy you a present!"

From a group of students I worked with for five days:

"Thank you for all the motivation and support you gave me"

"Thanks for all your support as well as teaching me new skills"

"You've changed my life. Thank you."

"You're an amazing man and you helped us a lot. You made me believe in myself more."

"Eric Cantona was a creative and revolutionary footballer, but you Eric (can't remember your second name) are even more creative and revolutionary."

"Hey Eric. I'd like to thank you for this wonderful week. You helped me a lot, especially with my confidence. I'll never forget this. Again, thank YOU!!!"

"A mass amount of effort that you put into each and every day. Thank you so very much."

"Once again – AMAZING! Thank you for all your hard work with the students".

"Thank you for your help with developing my skills. I know they will help me in the future, thanks to you".

"Throughout this week, our skills and confidence have developed in a way we didn't think possible. You're guidance has had an impact on the ways we see ourselves. We hope you NEVER forget us"

To Whom it May Concern

Ref: Mrs Suzanne F Gortler – Godalming Town Council

I have worked for Godalming Town Council for 8 years and had reached the point at where I needed to have some serious coaching about how to move myself forward. My line manager and the Councillors agreed that I could undertake training with Eric on a 1-1 basis. From the moment I sat with Eric, he understood my stumbling blocks, he listened and was able to provide practical and real-time strategies that have helped me enormously in the last (nearly a year) since I undertook my coaching with him. His coaching session and subsequent catch up discussions since the initial coaching have been invaluable to me. What I have learned from Eric has improved my professional outlook to such a degree that I have just been offered and accepted a large promotion within my organisation.

I feel that this might not have readily been offered if I had continued without Eric's Coaching.

I am grateful to Eric and hope that everyone might have the benefit of his coaching as it really has made a difference.

Thank you Eric.

Suzie Gortler
(Was Projects Coordinator for Godalming Town Council, will be undertaking the Communications Officer and Community Services Officer Role in two months)

CHAPTER 11

—

ERIC'S ONE LINERS

During my coaching sessions, there are many occasions when a one-liner comes in very useful to add clarity to what is being discussed. A great example of this is when I'm coaching someone who is not confident, and when we're talking about things that need to change in their lives, they use words like "hopefully" or "maybe" or "I'll try".

I then talk about my mentor in the States who taught me "Change begins with language". So, I get the person being coached to change the words that they are using. Instead of "hopefully", I might get "definitely" or "it will".

So, here are 54 one-liners that I use whenever the need arises during my coaching sessions:-

- "If it's to be, it's up to me"
- "Change begins with language"
- "You become what you believe"
- "If you think you can, you can. If you think you can't, you can't. But either way, you're right".
- "Don't beat yourself up"
- "Sometimes life just takes over"
- "We become what we think about"
- "Things happen for a reason"
- "It's meant to be"

- "I wish I had. I'm glad I did"
- "Nobody cares how much you know until they know how much you care"
- "You become the average of the five people you spend most of your time with"
- "Coaches focus on future possibilities, not past mistakes"
- "If you always do what you've always done, you'll always get what you've always gotten".
- "Be interested and not interesting"
- "Because you have to think anyway, you might as well think Big"
- "Think little goals and expect little achievements. Think big goals and win big successes"
- "FEAR. False evidence appearing real"
- "A year from now you may wish you had started today"
- "Success comes in cans, not cannots"
- "Aspire not to have more, but to be more"
- "Don't judge each day by the harvest you reap, but by the seeds you plant"
- "Completion rather than perfection"
- "People don't buy coaching, they buy their dreams. Sell dreams, not coaching"

- "You don't have to be great to get started, but you have to get started to be great"
- "You miss 100% of the shots you never take"
- "A coach is your beacon during stormy times"
- "You have greatness inside of you"
- "You are a winner"
- "There's nothing more powerful than a great idea whose time has come"
- "A person without confidence is like a jumbo jet sitting on a runway with an empty fuel tank"
- "All behaviour is belief driven"
- "My inspiration was my desperation"
- "Don't let school get in the way of your education"
- "Imagination is more powerful than knowledge"
- "Improve your brain, improve your self esteem"
- "Reasons reap results"
- "People remember what they see, not what they hear"
- "What I hear I forget; what I see I remember; and what I do I understand"
- "If you want to change something in your life, you've got to change something in your life".
- "There is no learning without remembering"

- "It's your attitude, not your aptitude, that determines your altitude"
- "You learn more from your mistakes than your successes"
- "Whatever the mind can conceive & believe, it can achieve"
- "People who are optimistic, accomplish more" - Thomas Leonard
- "Use GOALS as a way of keeping your VISION clear and visible" – Thomas Leonard
- "Winners are ordinary people with extraordinary determination."
- "If your action inspires others to dream more, learn more, do more & become more, you are a leader"
- "Success is the ability to go from one failure to another with no loss of enthusiasm" – Winston Churchill
- "Some people want it to happen, some wish it would happen, others make it happen".
- "People do not want to be sold a product or service. They want to deal with people who they think have their interests at heart or who care about them" – J.Oliver Crom, CEO Dale Carnegie
- "Aspire not to have more, but to be more"
- "Reasons reap results"
- "Yesterday is history. Tomorrow is a mystery. Today is a gift and that's why it's called The Present".

CHAPTER 12

—

IN CONCLUSION......

When I first started to write this, my first book, I was very clear in my own mind that I wanted to share my knowledge, gained over the past seventeen years, with as many people as possible, from as many countries as possible, around the world. I have always wanted to be the person that helps other people move forward with their lives so that they reach their true potential. This could have been seeing young footballers receive my coaching to become better, physically, tactically and mentally, or seeing young students in a school find out more about themselves, and realise that they actually had a lot more life skills than they believed they had.

My one-to-one coaching over the years, whether it was coaching a ten year old, or even a fifty year old, has taught me that it doesn't matter what the issue is, as long as one applies the relevant tools described in this book, then a solution can be found to move that person forward. Hopefully, the person being coached has come up with that solution in order to empower them to make sure that the action needed takes place. However, if the coach has had to help in some way, then this is fine.

My most recent experience of going into a school, one day a week, to coach a maximum of eleven students in a day, aged 16 to 19, on a one-to-one basis, all with different issues, has taught me a lot about the power of coaching, and why I had to write this book, so that others could use the "Eric Gilston coaching process" to help others.

I could write a whole book on this latter experience, but suffice to say, that what I have seen in one school, I would imagine is replicated throughout all schools, both primary and secondary, in many countries, and the need for coaching is paramount.

The key issues that these students were facing included stress, anxiety, depression, self-belief, confidence, anger and lots more personal ones that I will not mention as it could easily identify them. However, in the majority of cases, the issues stemmed from their early home life.

The fact that I was able to talk to these students about how these issues were affecting their lives, using the tools mentioned in this book, we were able to find solutions that have moved them forward to a life that is full of hope, and not despair based on their minds constantly recalling the past.

There are some instances where students need to see a counsellor or a therapist, and some where the need is for both the coach and the counsellor/therapist. In my view, this is an area where a lot more research is needed to clearly define what type of help is needed, depending on the issue(s) being faced by the student. The consequences for students not seeing the right person, and the frequency that they see that person, are quite horrendous, resulting in self harming and thoughts of suicide.

As a life coach, I learned from the students what their current issue was, and then proceeded to discover when this would occur, before discussing with them how they thought they could overcome it. So, let's look at a particular example from two perspectives, and see how you react to what I am saying.

A student tells you that they have an anger issue that has arisen from the way that their parents treated them from an early age. Do you get them to talk to you in detail about all the times when, as a child, they were mistreated by the parents OR do you talk to them about their current anger problem and when it occurs?

Think about this carefully, and see which route you would take and why. I'll come back to this later on.

You see, that in life, we always have 'choices' to make. Some may call it 'decisions'. In actual fact, I've heard it said, that we make about 500 decisions per day. Depending on which decision you make each time will determine the life that you will have. So, don't look to blame others for the life that you have currently, because you have made the decisions to get you to where you are today.

Some people see the glass as half full, and some see it as half empty; some people are positive while some are negative; some look for the good things in life and some look for the bad things, etc. Which person are you, and are you happy being that type of person?

So it is with my coaching. I would not have clients if everyone thought the same, and looked at things in a totally positive way. Therefore, when I get a client, it is clear to me that my role is to help them understand that there are lots of different ways to look at the same problem.

As I have said earlier on in this book, I see myself as a non-directive coach, and therefore initially I want to help the client look at their current situation from different ways to those that they have done to date. The great shame in life is that we are not taught these techniques early on, and if this had been the case, there would not be so many people with issues that they feel are insurmountable.

What I love about the coaching, and getting clients to open their minds to alternative ways of looking at their issue, is just watching the expression on their face, as they come up with new solutions to something that they have put up with, in many cases, for many years.

As I have said earlier on in this book, "the mind is very powerful", and I believe that I have heard, we only use about 0.1% of our brain cells. So, wouldn't it be nice, if we had a world where, whenever someone is faced with an issue, they immediately say to themselves "what are all the different ways that we could tackle this issue?" Not only would we open our minds to more possibilities, but we would start to use more different brain cells and we would realise just how powerful our mind really is.

If you have got this far in reading my book, then I would say you are a person who, in their heart of hearts, is serious about wanting to help other people move forward with their lives. So don't delay, go and find someone who has an issue that has been bothering them, and offer to work with them in order to find some new approaches that move them forward to resolve that issue. Use whatever tools you have read about in this book that you believe are appropriate, and see what works for you and what doesn't.

We all have to start at some time, so why not NOW? Who would have thought that in the year 2000 when I decided to start a Life Coaching course that the next seventeen years would give me so much pleasure that I would want to write a book?

If you do go ahead and start to coach, using one or more of the tools in this book, I would love to hear from you, telling me about your feelings both during and after your coaching sessions. As for me, I am looking forward to running my next coaching session in two days time, and I sincerely hope that you get to that stage when you feel exactly the same.

Bye for now. Good luck.

34635684R00059

Printed in Great Britain
by Amazon